We versus Them Equals Us

Inter-group Relations and
Social Identity Under Threat
in the Netherlands.

Juan E. Sarmiento Rodríguez

AT THE EDGE PUBLISHING HOUSE
LANCASTER, CALIFORNIA/
AMSTERDAM, THE NETHERLANDS

This book is dedicated
with much affection
to

my brother **Juan José Sarmiento,**
a scholar who has inspired me to live
in a way which is committed to others.

and

to pap and ma **Van der Caay,**
" My Dutch" parents,
who with their acceptance
took me safely by the hand on the journey
of learning "their culture",
which now has become part of mine.

CONTENTS

INTRODUCTION

The announcement of the Amsterdam mayor about the possible unrest of Moroccan youth and the recent riots in France and other European countries are good examples of the tense social relations between different ethnic groups and their "European countries of residence." An important question raised about these events is: How is it possible that the immigrants who want to live and grow in the West seem to be turning against its societies? The recent Australian riots against Arabs is another worrisome example of inter-group friction taking place around the world. These are situations in which groups have behaved aggressively against people with whom they have previously peacefully co-existed. They suddenly have started seeing each other as enemies. Social Psychology suggests that feelings of threats, related to personal and group identity experienced by nationals and immigrants, play the major role in these intricate social situations.

An individual experiences stress when confronted with different situations and people from other groups. This can generate a sense of threat that challenge them to "re-think" who they are and how they interact with other groups. Human beings can feel either secure or threatened when perceiving themselves as "insiders" of a group. These feelings of belonging or threat help them to maintain references about how they deal with others.

How does this all work? The Social Identity Theory (Turner & Brown, 1978; Tajfel 1972 and Turner, 1975, 1978b in Jetten Spears & Manstead, 1999) explains these processes as they are related to an individual's identity. The violent and non-violent behavior derived from these processes has also been studied using theories of social threat (Green, Glaser, & Rich; 1998; Pettigrew, 1998a). In both of these theories, the "context" of social behavior is an extremely important factor.

In the case of the Dutch social landscape, these theories offer insights that could help explain the group dynamics of its residents. They are important when trying to predict, analyze or prevent conflicts among different social and ethnic groups. When "categorizing" themselves, group members tend to make allegiances to different groups at specific moments. They use them as guides when trying to understand their place in society. These allegiances, together with salient current events in the World (e.g. September 11th, the assassination of the film director Van Gogh, the Madrid bombings, the war in the Middle East, etc.), underlie the tensions experienced by members of different groups.

This book offers a social psychological explanation to how adopting a specific group identity in the Netherlands can cause feelings of threat. It explains the kind of reactions groups have towards one other and how animosity between groups can shape the identity of Dutch citizens--both native and immigrant. These social psychological insights could help to improve the current social relations among nationals and immigrants in the Netherlands.

In this work, a summary of the "Threat Theories" (Green, Glaser, & Rich; 1998; Pettigrew, 1998a) aims to explain the reasons why people behave in a particular way when confronted with other groups. Additionally. The taxonomy made by Ellemers, Spears and Doosje (2002) will be used as a way to understand behavioral reactions to threat. The Social Categorization and Social Identity Theories (Turner et al., 1978) are used to explain how feelings of threats shape people's identity within the framework of the current Dutch context. These theories offer a good framework to describe the behavior of the individuals and of the collective of native Dutch and immigrant populations during the last few decades.

This work has five sections. The first one is dedicated to explain "Social Threat theories". The second explains the

"Social Identity Theory" and the "Self–categorization theory". The third section gives a brief socio-historical overview of the relationship between these two groups in the Netherlands. The fourth adds an explanation of the current situation using the theories already outlined. This describes how complex the formation of social identities attempts to be of help in understanding current events in the Netherlands. The last part offers conclusions and suggestions for improving of inter-group relations.

CHAPTER ONE

SOCIAL THREAT THEORIES:
IDENTITY AT SIEGE

Recently, Dutch newspaper headlines announced that two-thirds of Dutch natives have limited or no contact with their foreign neighbors [1].The immigrant population of the Netherlands reaches 10% of its inhabitants.They live mainly in big cities where the proportion of immigrants to Dutch natives is one to one. These statistical facts come from a government's report (Social and Cultural Planning Department, 2005) which was prepared to understand the present situation among the different groups that make up Dutch Society.

Until recent years, the Netherlands has been a relatively good functioning and tolerant "multicultural" society (Berry, Poortinga, Segall and Dasen ; 2003). However, after decades of immigration, this peaceful society has started to manifest sharp social tensions between groups, leading people to question the "apparent successes" of the political, social, economic, and immigration policies of the past. While they appear to have done little to help the integration of the new wave of new immigrants.

---

[1] *"Muslims in the EU:* Cities Report, The Netherlands. Preliminary research report and literature survey". pp. 22-23. Open Society Institute - EU Monitoring and Advocacy Program (EUMAP) (2007).

The tensions manifest themselves in different ways. One obvious way is that people now seem to express feelings of antagonism directly to members of other ethnic groups.

For social psychologists the feelings of social threat are described as processes that refer to inter-group biases. Social threats are described as perceptions of endangerment caused by others. The experimental observation and manipulation of social threats uses an instrumental distinction, splitting the construct "threat" into two levels. One level points to the perceived danger felt on an inter-group identity level. The other level points towards the perception of danger to the goals or positional hierarchy of the individual in relation to the groups.

Threats to identity can have different forms. For instance, Schachter (1959) studied the effects of threat at a personal level and demonstrated that people tend to affiliate with others who feel threatened. Another way is Pettigrew's (1998) who has based his study of Social Threat on Allport's Intergroup Contact Hypothesis work (Allport, 1954). In his explanation of threat he has asserted that increased anxiety and feelings of threat between groups become an impediment to good intergroup relations, making groups susceptible to develop negative relations.

Some groups also experience tensions of threat when their similarities are compared. Hewstone, Rubin en Willis (2002) observed that when social groups perceive that their similarities represent a threat to each other, they respond by trying to maintain or recover their distinctiveness. The perception of a group as being similar to other groups (or out-groups) threatens the group's social distinctiveness. In their attempts to recover their feeling of uniqueness, the members of groups may show hostile attitudes against others leading to acts of violence, crimes against minorities, hate crimes or even xenophobia.

Another model to describe threat is the proposal of "Integrated models of Prejudice", drawn by Stephan & Stephan (1993). Their central idea - based in the realistic group conflict theories (Bobo, 1988, Coser, 1956, Le Vine & Campbell, 1972; Sherif, 1966) - is that threat to identity leads to prejudice. This theory was called Intergroup Threat Theory (I..T.T.). The I.T.T. suggests that there are at least four types of threats: *realistic threats, symbolic threats, inter-group anxiety, and negative stereotypes.* Realistic threats refer to the economic and political power of the in-group along with perceived threats to the welfare of the group.

The symbolic threats refer to the perceived violation of in-groups symbolic beliefs. An example of this kind of threat may be the threat experienced by groups when norms and values (prescriptive and proscriptive) about how a society should function are questioned.

Related to group dynamics, the sensing of a threat has its origins when inter-group anxiety is felt, as it refers to the feelings of discomfort that people experience when anticipating or engaging in inter-group interactions. The anxieties caused during these interactions lead groups members to a reliance on cognitive heuristics and an amplified emotional reaction towards the members of out-groups. The so called negative stereotypes reflect the cognitive component of prejudicial attitudes towards out-groups, and may become evident when threats to the in-group are present.

Claude Steele (1997) has also defined a theory of threat focused on the individual, calling it 'Stereotype Threat'. His basic premise is that a person's "social identity"—defined as group membership in categories such as age, gender, religion, and ethnicity—has significance when rooted in concrete situations. Steele defines these situations as "identity contingencies" or settings in which a person is treated according to a specific social identity. In his research he points to the under performance of a person when a negative stereotype is attached to the social identity stereotype.

In a good intent to summarize the different literature about Social Threat, Branscombe, Ellemers, Spears and Doosje (1999) identify four different classes of threat. First, they mention a *categorization threat*, which relates to the assignment of stereotypical group characteristics to an individual group member. Sometimes, even against the person's own will. The second type of threat they describe is the *distinctiveness threat*. This is associated with not having a distinct social identity because it is prevented or undermined by outsiders who do not see a distinction. Thirdly, *threats to value*, which are defined by the tendency to protect the value of an important group membership when is directly attacked by an out-group. This kind of threat can enhance self-affirmation and self-stereotyping, and may be triggered by the competence or the morality of the group. Here the degree of identification of the individual with the group plays also an important role in the way the threat is experienced. The last class of social threat mentioned by Branscombe et al. (1999) is the *acceptance threat*. It refers to the feedback of the group on the individual and how he or she perceives him/herself to be accepted or not by the group. Being seen as a member of a group will affect the behavior of an individual in relation to other members of the group. All these four classes of threat are related to well presented social-psychological processes explained by the Social Identity Theory.

Identification with a group has also been reported by Branscombe et al. (1999) as having an effect on the group's experience of threat. In their research they reported that the awareness of how the different nuances of identification of the subject –high or low - with the group affects not only the experience of threat but also the person's responses to it. They noticed that the definition of a person's social identity in a specific context affects the content of the threat.

Another factor which importantly moderates the feelings of threat is the status of the group. This has been demonstrated by the tendency in members of low status groups to show more out-group favoritism (Jetten, Spears, & Manstead, 1999; Karasawa, 1995; Simon, 1992). When low status groups (such as minorities) try to obtain a positive social identity the feelings of threat appear when they are categorized as members of a different group, which they prefer not to be identified with. The members of the threatened group will prefer to change their status, and will tend to regard the out-group as more homogeneous than their own in-group. These members could also appeal to the distinctiveness of their in-group in order to "re-locate" themselves in a more positive scope or situation.

Stephan and Stephan (2001) have added a "typification of threat" to the subject, as they relate it to two types of dangers, namely, a *real* danger and *symbolic* danger. Real threat is related to the perception of situations where threat is imminent, whereas Symbolic threat is a consequence of feeling inferior as member of a low status group. Referring to groups members of low status groups, Simon (1992), has found that they are more likely to move along dimensions which are not primarily related to the status differential. The acknowledgment of in-group homogeneity along with a "status-defining dimension", highlights the inferior characteristics of the in-group.

Ellemers and Van Rijswijk (1997) found, in an experiment with a minimal intergroup situation (2), that members of a high-status group perceived greater in-group homogeneity than those of low status groups, regarding their status-defining (important) traits. They found the contrary when traits were status-irrelevant. These findings point to the next section of this paper, in which the Social Identity Theory is used to explain how the perception of the dimensional specificity of

---

[2] A research situation in which people are categorized on trivial basis, into groups without basic history.

homogeneity in groups leads people to different reactions when confronted with different types of threats. This becomes evident in situations when members of low status groups are perceived as having more in-group homogeneity, or when the intrinsic need for distinct social identity is perceived as being threatened (Simon & Brown, 1987; Doosje, Ellmers, & Spears, 1995; Ellemers & Van Rijswijk, 1997).

Another important type of threat is the threat to the intrinsic need for distinct social identity, triggering a perception of in-group homogeneity among the members of low status groups (Simon & Brown, 1987; Doosje, Ellmers, & Spears, 1995; Ellemers & Van Rijswijk, 1997). When this happens at an in-group level, the coherence of the group provides "entitativity", or in-group homogeneity perception, which helps the members of groups to acquire a sense of group distinctiveness.

Doosje and Kateman (2004) have presented threats in a simple way. They differentiate between the threat directed against the person (personal threat) or against the group (group threat). For them the causes of threat are rooted on the salience these have for the individual and in relation to the group in which the person belongs. They also found that members of individualistic groups (focused on the good of the individual) experience threats to the person in a stronger way than people from collectivistic groups (focused on the good of the group). Conversely, collectivistic group members perceive stronger group threat than personal threat in negative group contexts.

Threat Categories according to Ellemers, Spears and Doosje (2002).

As mentioned earlier, Branscombe et al. (1999), Ellemers, Spears and Doosje (2002) have summarized different ways of understanding threat. They use a taxonomy which displays the possible responses and strategies of the individual, relating these to the existing interaction between the commitment to group identity and the social context. Consequentially social situations derive from the interactions which are directly related to threats to identity (Spears et al. 1999, Turner, 1999).

Looking at the figure of the next page it is possible to say that a person located on the cell one (1) will not experience any threat to the self or to the in-group.
The answer of such individual having a low group commitment would be "noninvolvement", or no real social involvement. This individual sees himself simply as belonging or not belonging to the group without really feeling threatened. The individual may or may not share

personal and instrumental motives, rather than motivations and affects.

FIG 1. Threat Categories according to Ellemers, Spears and Doosje (2002)

	Group commitment	
	Low	**High**
No threat	**1.**	**2.**
Concern:	Accuracy/efficiency	Social Meaning
Motive:	Non-involvement	Identity expression
Individual-directed threat	**3.**	**4.**
Concern:	Categorization	Exclusion
Motive:	Self –affirmation	Acceptance
Group- directed threat	**5.**	**6.**
Concern:	Value	Distinctiveness, value
Motive:	Individual mobility	Group affirmation

On the same figure, any individual located on cell two (2) would experience a greater identification with the group than with his personal identity. This is shown when an individual demonstrates visible affective and behavioral responses as a way to affirm the individual's own identity, identifying him or herself with the in-group. This affirms the subject's identity in a group, differentiating his/her group from others. Here, threats to identity are not considered as urgent, because the context is not a source of threat to the group.

On cell three (3) the person is categorized by others as a member of the group. The threat, in this case, takes place when the categorization of the individual as part of the group activates perceptual, affective, and behavioral responses. These responses follow the desire of the subject to affirming his/her own personal or alternative identities, which may be considered different to the in-group's. This "resistance against" categorization does not automatically mean he/she rejects to be categorized in general.

Cell four (4) shows how a person who is committed to a group could feel threatened when he/she is excluded from the group. The person who finds himself in this type of situation will experiment negative affects, resulting in attempts to gain acceptance by trying to be in conformity with the group.

Cell five (5) shows the case of an individual who is not committed to the group and who only will be threatened when others assign negative value to his group. The tendency here will be to try to protect the individual who may then seek an alternative social identity.

In cell six (6) the threat is directed to the group level and the members of the group who are highly committed to it. These threats to value and to group distinctiveness can cause perceptual, affective, and behavioral reactions. These all aim to re-enhance of the integrity of the group, resulting in a high degree of self-stereotyping. This kind of individuals are highly committed group members, who could cultivate negative traits and behaviors as they procure to underline their distinctiveness from the out group members.

The taxonomy of Ellemers et al (2002) show that there are consequences to the way a person is categorized, and these cause an individual to behave in different manners. This is the main reason why the social identities of individuals play important roles in inter-group relations.

Summarizing this chapter, identities affect individuals, depending on the way they feel related to the in-group and threatened by the out-groups. Different theories of threat related to the way identities are perceived have been mentioned in order to introduce Chapter two, which explains the different attitudes and interactions of the diverse groups represented in the Dutch society, through the perspectives of the Social Identity and the Social Categorization Theories. These two theories are helpful to explain why people in Holland feel threatened in their identity as members of this nation, and how this society works for the preservation of its various identities, and the formation of new ones.

CHAPTER TWO

THE SOCIAL IDENTITY AND SELF CATEGORIZATION THEORIES

As showed in the previous chapter, individuals experience threats to their identities when confronted with members of other groups. These threats take different forms when an individual decides to categorize him or herself into a group, affecting the way he or she makes sense of his or her identity in the midst of society. An excellent theory used to explain these processes is the Social Identity theory (Tajfel; 1972). It refers specifically to the way people conceptualize themselves in inter-group contexts. People can then define themselves in relation to what they represent in their society. The Social Identity theory emerged as an extension to the explanations and the studies developed by Henri Tajfel (1972), after the research he made with his colleagues on Human Social Identity (Tajfel, Flament, Billing & Bundy, 1971). This theory explains how the value that the individual ascribes to a social group, and the value given to his sense of belonging to a group, are significant ways to understand how group memberships "shape" social and group relations. Individuals relate to members of their own group and to members of other groups, deriving their social identity from the evaluative properties of the group or groups which the person feels he or she belongs to.

A basic assumption of the Social Identity Theory, as explained by Tajfel & Turner (1986), is that groups and their members procure to enhance and protect positive distinctiveness and maintain a positive social identity (J.C. Turner 1975). These two phenomena display themselves clearly when a minimal formation of groups–minimal inter-group situation- is perceived, leading to self categorization processes which take place at different levels of a person's identity (Haslam, Oakes, Reynolds, & Turner, 1999; in Ellemers, Spears & Doosje; 1999) .

Three important aspects of the Social Identity Theory have been pointed by Tajfel (1979). The first he points at is the psychological analysis of the cognitive–motivational processes, leading to the need for a positive social identity. The second aspect is the elaboration of the analysis and the application to real inter-group relations, described as a continuum. This continuum goes from an inter-personal and individual point and runs to an opposite side, or the side of the inter-group relations – and vice versa. The third aspect is the explanation of the different levels of these processes which Turner (1978a, 1982, 1984) explains using the *Self Categorization Theory*.

In the Self Categorization Theory, Turner (1978a) elaborates further on the definition of the self of an individual who is related to a social context. The definition of the self - located at a specific point between the extremes of the inter-group relations continuum - mark the personal abstraction of the social levels of the categorization processes for the individual. These extremes are equidistant. One extreme is manifested when the individual "depersonalizes him or herself" in reference to the group. Here, the behavior becomes more referent to the group, and the personal level of reference fades away. In this case, the individual becomes more integrated and consensual as a member of the in-group. While this occurs, the behaviors of out-groups members are perceived by the individual as homogeneous (to the out group) and undifferentiated. This makes the person seek distance and differentiation from the out-group. The self exclusion of his or her personal identity from the out-group helps the subject to adapt and conform to the behavior of the group he has decided to categorize him or herself in (in-group). Not being part of the out-group helps a person define his or her personal identity.

According to Tajfel and Wilkes (Tajfel & Wilkes 1963, in Tajfel & Wilkes 1963, in Ottaway, Hayden, & Oakes, 2001) the accentuation of the within-group similarity and between-group difference lead group members to self-stereotyping and depersonalization of the self-perception. It is at this point when people use salient social categorizations to "be counted" as part of the in-group, and discounted as part of the "others, or out-group. The salience of a specific social identity would confer the group members the feeling that they are more "prototypical" members of the in-group, leaving aside their own individual identity. A suggestion derived from here is that the self of a person can adopt different identity- social or personal - depending of the salience of the level of categorization needed in a specific situation. The product of these "flexibility of the self" would be the personalization or depersonalization of the self-perception, bounded to the specific way the situation is perceived. The in-group becomes a "psychological reality", perceived as a reference to the self, as the person is confronted to "others". In the words of Turner himself:

> *"Personal identity refers to self-categories which define the individual as unique person in terms of their individual differences from other (in-group) person. Social identity refers to social categorizations of the self and others"*
> *(Turner 1999, in Ellemers et al. 1999, p)*

Self-categorization also has four main motivational components, namely, common fate, self-esteem, self verification and optimal distinctiveness.

Common fate describes the basic way in which people provide their references or social orientations towards others. Only the fact of experiencing a common fate will be enough for groups to start forming or altering the perception of identity the members of a group. They become "categorized" with everyone else who has the same fate.

Self esteem, as another motivational component of the Self Categorization, is found in the interdependence with others who help the individual to maintain it. This becomes visible when the personal self-esteem of an individual gets influenced by the experience related to the benefits of group success – also its losses- even without having to contribute to them (Cialdini & Kendrik, 1976). On an individual level, Baumeister, Smart & Bodem (1999, p. 241) have defined self-esteem as a favorable global evaluation of the individual, implying prestige, admiration, public esteem, respect and love. However, it also implies negative aspects of it, such as pride, egotism, arrogance honor, conceitedness, narcissism and sense of superiority. These negative aspects lead to aggressive behavior. Baumeister et. al (1999) affirm that high self esteem is a source of negative reaction and violence towards those threatening the ego of the person. These observations are in line with the different Theories of Threat mentioned in this paper, which generally propose that more aggressive behavior will be shown when the perception of threat for the individual or the group increases. When referring to specific situations, social and personal identities can vary in subjective importance, value, as well as chronic and situational accessibility. In short, emotional and behavioral consequences are attached to the individual in-group identification, especially when a person feels his or her group is being endangered by the out-group.

The motivational component *Self-verification,* points to the drive in subjects for establishing and maintaining a coherent self-image (Swann 1987). People have the tendency to resist changes to their own self-concept in order to maintain consistent self-appraisals. Hogg and Abrams (1993) have explained that this need for self-definition is central to the motivational basis for social identification. It helps to reduce the uncertainty when a person feels he or she belongs to a group. This need for inclusion is accompanied by a need for differentiation. This combination of Self-esteem and Self-verification has been called *"Optimal distinctiveness"* (Brewer and Brown, 1998). It is a combination which causes very powerful motivations defined by two important social effects, namely, *Assimilation and Contrast.* These two effects need to stay in balance in order to avoid perceptions of threat, guaranteeing people inclusion into the in-group, as well as differentiation from the out-group. Otherwise, the response could be an incremental preference for distinctiveness inside his or her own in-group (Pikket, 2002a). When feeling threatened, differentiation is activated in a way that social identification and in-group favoritism increase in order to defy the opinion or position of the out-group. A good example of this is visible among members of a minority group who are, because of the small size of their group, often associated as having "less power" than members of majority groups. In spite of its small size, the minority remains convinced of the worth of the cause it represents.

Referring to the status or situation of the groups, a group will cause its members to seek the improvement of their own personal situation. When the group realizes its disadvantageous position in relation to other groups, its members will tend to change their personal status in relation to the group when possible. A possible "subjective path" may offer a chance to "psychologically permeate" the boundaries, stability and legitimacy of the out-group. This perception may be the way individuals get their "chance to change" their status, personal situation, or even their group situation. This affects directly the way the group members relate to the members of both in-group and out-group. Other outcome of this group situation will be that members of the high status group may behave highly discriminatory against out-group members, feeling legitimated to do so because they feel threatened by low status members, in order to try to affirm their high status.

As seen here, the Social Identity Theory has the goal of offering explanations as to how the stereotyping process in terms of Self Categorization takes place. This explanation goes beyond other established models of prejudice, which - according to Turner (*Turner 1999, in Ellemers et al. 1999*)- have tended to be used as plain explanations to inter-group relations, without taking the importance of their social contexts into account.

In the following chapter the context of the groups relations in the Netherlands will be presented in a socio-historical way, reviewing the developments of the forming of the tensions between the two groups: The Dutch Nationals and the Immigrant group. Both are central players when trying to understand the current social relations in the country and the origin of the social threat perceived by both of them. After chapter three, chapter four will aim to apply intergroup theories of threats to the interpretation of the Dutch context and its social relations.

CHAPTER THREE

"Us" versus "them": Social Groups and Group's relations in The Netherlands

Verkuyten (2001) researched how the behavior of ethnic minorities (or out-groups) residing in old Rotterdam's neighborhoods were considered "abnormal" by Dutch nationals (in groups). In his research, Verkuyten examined the discourse of ethnic Dutch residents in the inner neighborhoods of Rotterdam. He points at the way how people's versions of reality and their selfs are based on the comparison of themselves with other groups. This comparison requires the construction of a specific version of reality as well as the categorization of in and out-groups. Verkuyten found that the distinction between two groups - "them" and "us", made local people feel better and "different than the others or the foreigners". This is an clear example of the current state of affairs in the Netherlands. People live beside one another, yet they feel they belong to different groups. In their need to make sense of their social environment, every individual needs to make a social map that directly affects not only themselves, but everybody else in their surrounding as well. But in which extent this applies to the Netherlands?

Different social groups make up the contents of an individuals social map. Hogg, Abrams, Otten and Hinkle, (2004), have defined social groups as "a collection of more than two people who have the same social identity". This means that almost everything a person feels identified with at a specific moment and in conjunction with other people, can make people consider themselves as forming part of a group. The stress perceived in inter-group relations create feelings of threats which now seem be shaping the social identities of people living in the Netherlands.

Categorization processes lead automatically to the perception of the out-groups, as identities rely on the social categorizations made by people in relation to the social context. Significant events such as rapid demographic changes, the attacks of the Twin Towers in New York on September 11th, the so called "War on Terrorism", the European Union integration, economic stagnation or the terrorist attacks that took place in some European cities, have worked together in forming the context that have made people more aware of gaps and differences between groups in society. As these things happen, each member of a group tries to make sense of its social reality using social categorization. As proposed by the Social Identity theory, individuals try to see similarities with their in-group, as well as their differences with other groups. According to Hoog (Hogg, 2000), groups in society seek to shape their collective self through achieving or holding on to a positive inter-group distinctiveness. This sets the formation of both individual and collective identities in a central place to understand group's dynamics.

In the view of J. Howard (2000) there are important social bases for the formation of individual and collective identity. He has mentioned six major social bases in which groups could be generally identified with, namely, ethnic identity, sexual identity, gender identity, class identity, identities of (dis)ability and age identities. This paper refers mainly to ethnic identity, which as psychological construct relates mainly to the theoretical research on ethnic identity formation. Ethnic identity formation includes components of ethnic identity and the findings on self-esteem, self–concept, ethnic adjustment, ethnic identity in relation to the majority, as well as changes related to immigration. The analysis of the two main groups represented in the country (the Dutch Natives and the Non-Dutch residents) is base of used in this paper as a mean to point at the way Dutch people have organized their identity until recently, and how other groups have socially developed in the country.

Pre-immigration time: Dutch Verzuling and Societal Changes

Pillarization has been a useful term coined by the Dutch social researchers Arend & Lijphart (Arend Lijphart, 1968) and, until recently, used as a way to describe social group relations in the country. The concept is used to refer to the way social groups have formed, at least in the last two centuries of the Netherlands. According to Spiecker en Sleutel (2001), these "pillars" were constituted by social and religious groups or "zuilen (in , Dutch)". Groups in the Netherlands have gelled together around own comprehensive and moral doctrines, forming what in Dutch has been conceptualized as "zuilen", or social structures that shaped the bases on which the segmentation of Dutch society has construed itself. Pettigrew & Meertens (1996) describe this Pillarization (verzuiling, in Dutch) as the system Dutch society has coordinated and distributed its resources. In their opinion, it has been a remarkable way of organizing groups which – differing from other countries- has eased up inter-group conflicts.

These "verzuilings" or groups forming pillars were formed in a more or less "culturally homogeneous" country than the current Netherlands has become. At that time, this was the way groups organized themselves in order to be represented, bringing forth their representatives to society. They received all the support of the group's members with the goal of to representing their interests. These men or women held the group's authority in order to strategically position their groups in the different influential social-political networks of the country (Van der Horst, 2001). Representatives were also allowed to manipulate their groups as they leaded them. In that way, the participation of large groups of the population at the social, political and economical levels of the nation was guaranteed. Protestants, Catholics, Liberals and Socialists groups unwinded into and participated in this "pillarized country". They sustained a model of what was denoted as *'consensual democracy'*. This organization of society has appeared successful in its softening of tensions among different groups. But it has been far from perfect, because of the permanent but less evident tensions among social groups. Apparently the tensions were then less visible, and this may be the reason why Meertens and Pettigrew, 1997 found a subtle racism in The Netherlands, in contrast to "blatant" racism that other countries have portrayed.

The 'verzuiling' brought effective emancipation to the different communities – especially the Christian. Even so, this model of organizing the country has eroded during the last three decades. Reasons for this erosion are found in the introduction of mass production, the increase of the incomes levels and the emancipations movements, among other factors.

Secularization and individualism (Pettigrew et al. 1996) have made their way through the Pillarization system, a "societal midfield" has been left behind (Spiecker and Sluitel, 2001). This caused people to feel disconnected from their groups in the system. It also left behind ideologically neutral organizations and institutions which were created to serve groups during the former system. Remarkably, even when they still function, these organizations do not serve their ideological origins, but instead they work as support for immigrants who assign their own content to the "loose and neutral institutions". An example of this are the different purposes given to the church or synagogue buildings now used as neighborhood centers, places to help immigrants, mosques, restaurants, and even museums or fancy offices.

Two Groups, One country: Immigrants and Natives
With the increasing influx of foreigners arriving to the country in the nineties, the number of non-western foreigners grew to about 1,5 million people, and by 1997 this meant 9,4% of the population (Spiecker & Sleutel, 2001). This movement of people coming from other countries has caused important demographic changes. The big cities have felt the weight of the influence caused

by the immigrants. Amsterdam is a vivid example of this, having by 2005 about 174 nations represented in it, and where 60 % of its inhabitants under twenty are members of a minority group.

This work, focuses on the two groups defined by the social dynamics and identities produced by immigration. The first group defined here is the majority group (Pettigrew 1998), or dominant group (B.Correnblum & Walter G Stephan, 2002 in Licata, L and Klein, O. 2004), which Doosje and Kateman (2004), referred to as the " Natural Dutch". They are those whose family roots are found in the country, and date to at least two generations. The second group is the Immigrant Group, formed by ethnic minority groups who were attracted by the prosperity of the country in the seventies. They first came from Dutch ex-colonies and the Mediterranean area, and later different groups from all over the world arrived. Even when the Netherlands has always accepted guest workers, it was after the Second World War, when people form South-European countries arrived. In the early sixties masses of people from Turkey and Morocco moved to the country, but about sixty percent of these workers returned to their own country. Those who decided to stay were welcomed and encouraged to bring their close relatives along. An important subgroup among the immigrants have always been those coming from industrialized nations such as Germany, United Kingdom, Japan, United States and Belgium. These "expats" were also attracted by the prosperity of the country, blending more easily into the culture of the Dutch.

Another important group of immigrants have been the refugees, who have always been welcomed since Holland has been a land with a great tradition of hospitality. As result, about 33.000 refugees had received legal status since the Second World War, and through the end of the eighties (Entzinger & Stijnen; 1990)

Pettigrew's analysis of European minorities assigns the immigrants to seven statuses (Pettigrew 1998). The first and more favored are the national migrants, coming back to the "forefathers land". The second are European themselves, who posses full rights, based on the European Union's agreements. The third status is the one of the ex colonial people, coming from other continents. Fourth, are the recruited workers, invited as guests to help in the strengthening of the national industries, and who formerly were expected to leave before developing family roots. The fifth group is the Refugees and asylum seekers group, which is highly diverse and difficult to define socially. The sixth status is given to those "accepted as illegal immigrants", who don't have papers or social welfare benefits, but are tolerated by the authorities. The last status is the one of "true illegal". These are those perceived as having economic needs and often deported. These people could form criminal groups, giving room for locals to generalize their activities as characteristic to "all immigrants".

The estimation is that more than 10% of the total population of this country is made up of immigrants or "first generation immigrants". This is why it has become necessary to re-conceptualize society into a "multicultural society model". This model aims to help organize the notable changes driving society towards pluralism and diversity. When talking about relations of the immigrants in this "multicultural model", Berry, Poortinga, Segall and Dasen (2003) have defined Multiculturalism as a temporary stage on the way to assimilation, which accepts both the maintenance of cultural identity and characteristics of ethno cultural groups, as well as the contact and identification of all in a large plural society. This approach to social organization has given The Netherlands a way to breach the gap left by the societal changes, giving directions to social relations. According to Bontje & Latten (2005) the 'non-Western' population grew from 160.000 in 1972, to 1,7 million in 2004. The estimate for 2005 points to 1.669.179 people, of first generation non-Western' population.

As the big cities have felt the societal impact of immigrants, the Dutch National group, have hoped for their 'spontaneous' economic and political integration, just as it had happened in the past with the "Pillarization model". The reality seems to have been different, making the integration into the Dutch society seemingly not successful. This situation has become an important political issue, because the two groups-Dutch and not Dutch- seem to have stayed away from each other. Social Categorization theory explains the complexity of these relations, because it proposes that people and groups compare each other by assessing the relative value of their in-groups and other "out-groups". The consequence of the comparison is a painful "We- They distinction" within the country.

The context in which immigrants who stay in the country find themselves creates a wide variety of identification degrees, making them to they show variable levels of identification (high or low) with other groups in society. In the case of the National Dutch, different aspects of identity such as language, color, perception of privilege, etc., could cause the triggering of more tensions. Deux (2000), together with Roccas and Brewer (2002) have underlined that the choosing for a group in society automatically defines one's identity, and such identity could always be threatened by others. As Ellemers et al.

(2002) have already explained it; individuals and groups show different responses when feeling threatened. In the next chapter, these theories are applied to the Dutch social reality, aiming to help with understanding the root of the problems and help ease tensions in this society.

CHAPTER FOUR

THREAT PERCEPTION AND SOCIAL IDENTITY

As seen in Chapter Three, The Netherlands has become a pluralistic society, and such societies frequently reflect inter-group conflicts. Social Identity Theory proposes that a dimensional specificity in homogeneity perception will lead the different reactions from group members, when confronted to threats to their identity. This is the result of inaccurate ways in which groups may perceive one another. Attitudes developed against groups can cause individuals to become more attentive to information relevant to group boundaries present in specific situations. This creates in people a more homogenous perception of both in-group and out-groups.

At an interpersonal level, Simon (in Hogg et al., 2004) has expressed that the "identities" of an individual, could be seen as different places an individual takes in society. A person could share different identities at different levels incorporating them into his or her self-concept. A person relating to his or her inner circle (few or exclusive group of people; e.g. family), may deal with a identity different than the one the same person uses relating to others with whom he or she shares a less intimate degree of identity. Different identities of the same individual are used in different situations. The arguments of Simon make it possible to speak about *'levels of conceptualization of an individual'* when explaining social relations and group dynamics. In other words, depending on how the person categorizes him or herself or is categorized by others, it will be expected that he or she will behave in certain way, in relationship with his in-group and out-group position. According to the Self Categorization theory, it is possible for an individual to assume simultaneous and maybe overlapping categories as he or she feels part of more than one group category. So, depending of the context one person finds him or herself, it will be possible to display different levels of social identity and self-categorization. But even this being the case, Social psychological analysis of identity will depart from the assumption that one situation can activate only one psychological real identity. Analyzing the complexity of identity in this way becomes a doable task, one psychological identity at the time.

Roccas & Brewer (2002) have further elaborated on the complexity of the Social identity, describing the way individuals are in capable of distinguish in-group and out-group members. This is connected to the way a person perceives his or her own set of different identities. Roccas et al. (2002) noticed that when group identities do not converge with the structures of the individual, the person tries to make sense of the new categorization using four strategies. The first is *Intersection*, or the definition of the in-group as a "compound or intersection" of multiple group membership. The second, *Dominance*, is a strategy in which the person's social identity precede all others. Here the individual considers all those who share his identity as in-group members. The third, *Compartmentalization*, is the strategy used when identities are linked to specific situations and context. Here the context decides the primacy of the identity. The last is the *Merger*, a strategy in which non-convergent membership are simultaneously recognized and embraced in the most inclusive form. This makes it possible to merge the identity of all groups together.

As said before , the context plays an important role as the "social (re)arrangement" or (re)definition of identities of different groups and their members in The Netherlands compare and contrast each other. Here is the place where individuals make use of their own 'levels of conceptualization' in order to quests for "self categorization", procuring to identify and commit with their in-groups. Deaux (2000) mentions multiple dimensions of social comparison Deaux (2000) which define the political, economical and cultural aspects as basis of comparison among groups. These three aspects function in both the inter-group as well as at inter-personal levels of group relations. At a personal level, the conceptualization of the self in relation with the groups becomes a vital referential for the shaping of the social identity of the individual. This "main point" offers some sort of "secure social identity", from which threats are perceived. Branscombe and Spears (2001) agree with this and say that the social behavior of individuals is not only a product of cognitive universals, but also a product of social contextual factors that assign meaning to a specific event. For Branscombe et al (2001) an *idiosyncratic* personality (or type "I") is that which is personally attributed and not shared with other people. This way of looking at inter-group relations simplifies the explanation of one particular identity, assumed by an individual in a specific context. At an inter-group level, identifying with a group helps with the formation of a *"collective self construal"* in this kind of specific situations.

In the case of the Netherlands, their long history, tradition and stability of this country gives the Dutch Nationals a broad point of comparison when they contrast themselves with the "just arrived" group of immigrants. Different, but classic dynamics of inter-group relations become visible as the nationals are asked about their views with respect to the new population, and conversely, when the immigrants are asked to describe the way they see their host country and their citizens. In many cases, the immigrant group is seen by the Dutch as retaining powerful attachments to their native cultures and as remaining gathered in bleak enclaves with their compatriots. Dutch Natives usually see newcomers as members of out-groups, causing the in-group bias well shown in the scarcity of contact among the Dutch Natives and immigrants. Immigrant groups show also in-group bias, but they possess a less stable basis of comparison than the Nationals. The immigrant minorities struggle to find out who they are, in a new context, trying to activate levels of conceptualizations of their different "selves" in reference to their group (in-groups), and in reference to others (out-groups). Their aim becomes seeking to be accepted in the host society without betraying their own identity. For instance, the research made by Timotijevic and Breakwell (2000) among immigrants from the former Yugoslavia in Great Britain showed the impact immigration had on their identities. They pointed to the "disruption" that takes place when a person moves to a different country. Major life changes take place, especially when leaving their countries in an abrupt way, and these "new comers" engage in different processes such as meaning-making, position negotiation and group categorization in order to regain their feelings of self-efficacy, distinctiveness, continuity and self-esteem. Emotional and cognitive processes are experienced by the immigrants These processes become critical points, through which, as the Social Identity Theory states it, the personal identification with a group (or many groups) will help defining who the individual is. The immigrant determines either he or she is a member or not of the in-group, in relation to the out-group. This decision will define the way he is supposed to behave. Threats to a person's own identity play important roles in defining identity and shaping identification in specific situations, helping the individual to trace out its allegiances and fidelities towards groups in society.

Another example of the groups dynamics was set by Long and Spears (1998; in Leach and Williams, 1999) in an experiment in which university students were told that they had been "less positively evaluated" by people of other groups. These individuals showed in-group favoritism while evaluating the work of out-groups, as a consequence of believing of they were being negatively evaluated. North Ireland is another example of these dynamics, where tensions among political and religious factions have been going on for decades. These are built on the perception of threat each group perceives from the other.

Main types of identity threats in Dutch Society

The different theories and taxonomies outlined in the chapters before help to predict the various ways groups could react to threats to their groups in the Netherlands. The reaction to feeling threaten by members of the two groups- Majority Dutch Nationals and Immigrants will always relate to the commitment to their own group and the way they perceive threat. Ellemers et al. (2002) mentioned four examples of the way group members could react when confronted with four real-threat scenarios.

1. **Direct Identity Threat, Low Commitment with the Group.** In the case of a *"Native Dutch" who has been directly threatened, but has low commitment with his group,* the threat will be directed to the performance of the in-group itself and its relation with the individual's self-esteem. A "Dutch native" who seeks to improve his/her self-esteem will feel threatened in his/her individuality when he/she, against his/her own will, perceives the risk of being treated as a prototypical member of his in-group. In this case, this person will be more concerned about the lost of his personal identity than about the in-group identity. As predicted by the Social Identity Theory, this out-group favoritism could be the consequence of the low commitment individuals considering the possibility of achieving a better status, if he/she could change his/her group membership. An example of this could be the case

of an individual who is used to working or living among people from different nationalities, and whose opinion, positive or negative - about the "immigrant group" may be different than the one of his in-group (Dutch Natives). He may feel the negative opinion of the in-group being "tacitly" forced upon him by others, pushing him to conform in a way that he assumes this opinion as being the same as theirs. In this case, the person will fear stop being faithful to himself, his own ideas and his uniqueness. These feelings of having an identity imposed by others, and determined by his affiliation to an in-group will not really represent him. As consequence, the person will try to create a richer definition of himself in order to counter a "non-desirable" categorization within the in-group. In other cases, he will purposely under perform as member of the group, in order to avoid being seen as prototypical of the group. When categorization is inevitable, the person whose high self-esteem is threatened will tend to display the in-group bias as an attempt to compensate for individual concerns.

An example supporting this is the experiment set by Guimond and Dambrun (2002), in which French students of psychology were led to believe that their own group (psychology students) was much worse off or much better off in terms of job opportunities than an out-group (students in law). The assessment of the perception of the standing of the two groups (cognitive elements) and the feelings associated with these perceptions (affective elements) revealed that the participants in the group with low performance condition expressed more discontent with the fate of their group than those in the control condition. Participants in the "good group performance condition" expressed greater feelings of satisfaction or gratification than the control group.

From the perspective of the immigrant, a member of this group who is directly threatened and has a low commitment to the group will tend to adapt better to thr host culture. The perception of threat to identity experienced will take place at the in-group level, meaning this also is a threat to his or her self-esteem (Branscombe et al. 1999). This immigrant whose identification with the in-group is not strong (may be a "second generation migrant" or immigrants) will try to find his or her way into the Dutch Society. This person will identify more with the local culture, and little with his ethnic, religious and family background. He or she will tend to seek opportunities to psychologically permeate the high status groups (Native Dutch) or create "subjective paths" as ways to change his status situation. This kind of individual will take any opportunity to try to be categorized among the out-group (Dutch Natives), because of his awareness of the low status of his in-group. These are people who have decided to "renounce" their homeland' s passport and have made their lives more similar to that the of the Dutch Natives. They feel more affiliated to the Dutch language, culture, values and tradition and using the words of Berry et al. (2003), they tend to be better "assimilated".

2. Directed Threat and High Group Commitment

The case of an individual experiencing *directed threat and holding on to a high group commitment*, with the in-group. This person will look for acceptance and be concerned about the possibility of being excluded from the group. Any perception of rejection from the members of the in-group will create negative feelings, bringing the individual to recognize the threat of having a peripheral status as member of the group. The person will seek to perform actions to compensate for this, but sometimes without admitting his or her peripheral position. On a behavior level, the person will try to portray the prototypical behavior of the in-group when visible to other members of his group. In extreme situations, the person could even show anti-social behavior depending on the relevance of the norms of the group. A good example of this are the so called "Lonsdale youth". These are Dutch youth influenced by nationalistic and extreme right wing propaganda, who behave according to these group's norm in order to feel they belong to the group. These kids have the same dress code (their name come from wearing the same brand of clothes: "Lonsdale") and perceive any person belonging to any different group as being a threat to their identity. With this dressing code, Dutch Natives with nationalistic ideas could derive their self-concept or roots from nationalistic or racial connotations.

In the case of an immigrant experiencing *directed threat and holding on to a high group commitment*, a threat will be when hearing that he or she does not represent the in-group. They will then present more in-group favoritism (Doosje & Ellemers, 1997) and will attempt to positively differentiate their in-group from the out-group. They also will feel threatened by feeling categorized by others as "non–prototypical" in-group members or "black sheep". These members are different in many important categories from the in-group. The subject will feel threatened in relevant categories to the identity of the immigrant such as language, cultural customs, behavior and religious practices typical to its group. An exemplification of this could be the relatedness of many of the Muslim immigrants to the Islamic practices, which define an important part of their identity. A member of the immigrant group for whose Islamic identity is very important will act according to the more strict rules of its religion. This could lead to strong criticism of non-prototypical in-group members. They feel threatened when they are told they do not represent (or are not prototypical to) the in-group, and can show high levels of out-group derogation. The "born again" Muslims, or extremist, reflect this reality. They seem to have re-encountered the "Pure Islam" after a period of identity crisis. They become the members of their religious group who are willing to sacrifice themselves -as individuals - in order to be seen as "real Islamic" believers (Roy, 2004) and to strengthen the group status.

3. Perceived threats to the group by a member with low commitment.

The threat to a group *perceived by a member with low commitment* will trigger in the subject a tendency to avoid association with any negative identity traits of the group. Due the low of identification with his group, the negative association with the group will not always be felt as a threat. The group's identity does not have a significant value, because the individual's self is not associated with it. This makes the particular identity of the person stronger than the group's. The negative reaction from others towards the in-group may not affect the person, but instead enhances the individual's self. Feeling of not as a holder of the prototypical features of the group, makes the person to report low levels of self-stereotyping. If an opportunity to switch to the identity of a higher status groups is given, the person will choose to move to the group which seems to be better off. This person will not do much to improve the condition of the in-group because he or she could abandon it at any time. Feelings of guilt Dutch studied by Doosje et al. (Doosje, branscombe, Spears, Manstead 1998) are a good example of this. In their research, Dutch natives were asked questions about the colonization of Indonesia by The Netherlands. The people who had less identification with the group showed less in-group variability in their perception of the group. Consequently, they showed less readiness to use group membership as basis for judgment on this issue.

For the immigrants who *perceive a threat to their group, but are members with low commitment,* their feelings will not be affected by the stereotype judgments about the group made by others. In an experiment made by Abrams and Hutchison (2002) low identifiers showed less cognitive resources than high committed members while processing information about a deviant group member. This demonstrates that the low committed members seem to be less worried about their in-group situation and status. This will happen when group membership tends to be more self conceptually important. The low committed member exhibits none or moderate responses when the group's prototype is ambiguous or threatened (Branscombe et al 1999). Consistently, people who know that their group is stigmatized (e.g. Moroccans, Muslims) may avoid being identified as a prototypical member of their in-group (e.g. Islamic).

4. Group-directed threat, high commitment.

Doosje and Branscombe (2003) found in their research that individuals who were highly identified with a group which behavior is considered as being negative, would ascribe this behavior to external attributes. When highly committed Dutch Natives feel a threat directed to their group, they will perceive the out-groups (immigrants, in this case) in a more homogeneous way. They will ascribe negative behavior to the internal attributes of the out group. A threatened high committed Dutch National will be prone to "consent" or even actively participate in the derogation of a different group, attributing this negative behavior to the "homogeneity of the out-group". An example to illustrate this is the "generalization of all Muslims" as terrorist, after the extreme Muslims terrorists' attacks. A highly committed member of the Native Dutch group would think that anyone who looks like a Muslim is a terrorist, justifying the use of violence and even discriminatory behavior against any member of the out-group. According to Pettigrew (1998), the settling of millions of people from other countries in Europe, and in the Netherlands, has caused four major reactions from locals, namely prejudice, discrimination, political opposition and violence.

People who hold extreme group stereotypes will procure to protect or restore the value of their in-group identity, because this value has important self-conceptual references to their identity. The presentation of a positive image will help to protect the in-group. The members will emphasize solidarity and commitment to the in-group in order to "restore the positive stereotypical value" of the in-group. They might also try to achieve cognitive and behavioral differentiation, leading to accentuated forms of stereotype formation. For instance, the rejection by the members of the Islamic community in the Netherlands (to which the majority of immigrants belong), avoiding identification with the terrorist attacks perpetrated in different parts of the world. They take distance themselves from these terrorists, and see them as people who have "deviated from Islam".

According to the taxonomic information given in previous chapters, the ideal situation in which both Dutch natives and immigrants could function positively will be in a non-threatening and high committed situation. This situation will allow the members of both groups to function being themselves, but without feeling the pressure of threats coming from another group. The challenge with such high committed group members is that the context, which is frequently not controllable, directly affects inter-group relations. Inter-group tensions may be revived due to an external and - even not directly related- international conflicts involving people who are associated to the identity of the groups. This is shown in the way the salience of religion and the so-called "War on Terror" have activated categorizations on both nationals and immigrants and ignited conflict and social unrest.

Behaviors caused by feeling of threat shown by different people in the Dutch context reflect difficult intergroup situations. Giving answers to help improving relations among groups in the country remains a complicated task. The closing chapter of this paper advocates for the calling forward of a "prototypical identity", common to all the "inhabitants of the Netherlands". This new "general identity"- framed into the socio-psychological theories previously mentioned- may help to re-categorize identities in the country, and in a way, to alleviate existing intergroup tensions.

DISCUSSION AND CONCLUSIONS

As said before, issues of categorization, identity and perception of threat are complex and affect group dynamics in the Netherlands. The theories of Social Identity and Social Categorization make it clear that individuals adopt diverse modes of identity depending on their context, emotional state and salience of their groups in society. As group allegiances set, identities become more visible, affecting dynamically the boundaries of group identification. This lays at the center of the causes for experiencing threats to identity, causing people to display forecasted behaviors, such as those described in the former chapter.

There is no doubt that coexistence between Immigrants and Dutch Nationals has been affected by the felt threats and subsequent behaviors. The perceptions of threats play an important role in shaping and forming the individual identities of the groups in the Netherlands. These experiences of threat lead people to evaluate and (re)categorize themselves based mostly on the antagonist perception of other groups. As described before, Social Identity Theory has used the commitment of people to their groups as a starting point, helping define identity at specific times and at different levels.

It remains important, however, to find punctual answers to the specific question of how the adopting of a specific group identity in the Netherlands can cause feelings of threat and tensions? Social Identity Theory offers an answer that to that question by relating it to the main moderators of tensions and in-group bias. These moderators are strength or commitment to the identification with the group, and the context in which the threat takes place. In other words, that there will be different reactions to threat corresponding to the level of commitment of the individuals to the group in any specific situation. For instance, a highly identified person will perceive more group deprivation, and as result, will react to recover privileges for his or her group. This will accentuate differences among groups. Reactions generated towards other groups could vary in intensity, starting from a sense of discrimination, reaching extreme expressions of violence and hate crimes against other groups.

These actual animosities caused by feelings of threat among groups affects relations, and seem to be shaping negatively the identity of all the Dutch citizens both of natives and of immigrants. At a group level, the motivational components of categorization processes such as common fate, self- esteem, self verification and optimal distinctiveness affect the experiences of threat., simply because threats can either enhance or weaken the identity of groups in society. The taxonomy of Ellemers et al. (2002) indicates that those whose identity will feel weakened are those with low or no commitment with their group (Cells 3 and 5 of the taxonomy, see table on page 9).

Other cause for the animosity between groups may be explained by the effects of Optimal Distinctiveness processes, which cause people - especially those who have a high sense of commitment with their group- to want to enhance their identity, and producing the restoration of balance in people's own identity as their goal after experiencing a threat. Here, again questions to help understand the situation in the Netherlands rise: what kind of balance is to be formed? What kind of identity needs to be supported in order to guarantee harmony in the country? Waters (1990, in Deaux 2000) offer a response by saying that self identification with a group is not biological or primordial, but involves a great deal of choices. According to Deaux (Deaux, 2000) identity becomes a subjective manner, a social construction that requires negotiation in order to choose for one of the options of identities which are offered in a particular moment. Threats from out-groups will cause in-group members to become more of one mind in order to enhance their identity.

Because national identity as social construction plays an important role in the life of any country, the promoting of a "common identity" could help the creation of a different "psychological reality", which will result in society drifting apart from conflict and improving groups relations. This may not be a simple enterprise, given all the different factions, challenges and influences affecting society and group dynamics. It is also necessary to recognize the danger that this proposed "ideal identity" may cause, if it degenerates, enforcing a type of "new nationalism" ruining inter-group relations. But the risk of offering a new national –without becoming nationalistic - identity is worth giving it a chance, in order to offer perspectives to "the new others", for a better self categorization into this "supra-identity" in which all the inhabitants of the Netherlands could participate and be included.

The idea is to promote a "prototypical" identity of the "inhabitants of the Netherlands" to which all could have a certain degree of affinity, and in which they can feel included. This identity would describe the ideal "Dutch citizen" subordinating other categorizations into it. For instance , it would be is interesting to measure the effects of an identity campaign recently designed by the city of Amsterdam is "I Am-sterdam", seeking to promote the identity of the city and its more than 150 nationalities represented. This was created in order to make people living in the city conscious and how they are part of the city. This campaign seems to have had a good effect on people, becoming a good example of re-categorizing the inhabitants of the city into a category in which they all feel they can belong to.

As presented by the Social Identity Theory, the re-categorization of individuals will help to be "absorbed into a Common Identity Model" (Gaertner, Dovidio, Anastasio, Bachma, & Rust; 1993) based on a "Common Dutchness" among the groups. This could also help subordinating the commitment to their in-group to their commitment to a Dutch identity. This "Common Dutchness" will make feasible the existence and good functioning of other subordinated identities based on any religious, ethnic, or geographic identities. The identities then, could become included into their "main" Dutch identity. This idea directly relates to what Urban & Miller, 1998 (In Roccas et al., 2002) have called the "Merger model" or the crossed categorization of groups. The proposed new national identity will be the result of combining the acknowledgement of immigrants as an active and equal part of the national community by the

Dutch Natives, and the acknowledgement by immigrants to become an integral part of the in-group. They both could therefore participate in the formation of a new national identity. In this way, immigrants will become part of the country as a whole, when asked to participate in the social dynamics.

It is clear that "other identities" could be made more salient in a specific context or situation, and special attention would be necessary in order not to leave any group outside "Dutch civic" (or Merger) identity. Not doing this may lead to feelings of not belonging, and to extreme positions, nationalistic ideas, and biased feelings, which would revive old conflicts, as group relations become derailed.

After all what has been explained here, it is possible to say that as long as groups in the Netherlands do not feel they have a "clear common identity" with the rest of the population , they will consider it important to hold and maintain a positive evaluation of their in-group (imbalanced distinctiveness). This will lead the groups to in-group favoritism in judgments and behavior. The recognition of "all" members of both immigrant and Dutch nationals groups is necessary, and it will be affected by the way they feel complemented by each other, creating a social map in which boundaries could be diluted. This can create positive attitudes and circumstances because of the intrinsic feelings of belonging and the need to be preserved from the threats presented by the other out-groups. If these are held continually and long enough, this strategy will determine the way people feel about themselves and therefore shape their social identity in relation to tolerance towards the other groups' members that make up Dutch society.

The old way of looking at the immigrant group as a "zuil" (pillar) without considering the possibility of them becoming part, can cause these immigrants or "New Dutch Citizens" to feel marginalized, making them feel that they are not part of the in-group. This could, in consequence augment inter-group differences. In extreme situations, the perception of homogeneity of the out-group can even deteriorate to the "depersonalization of out-group members", excluding any possibility of contact. The words of a radical Muslim interviewed by Jacobson (1997) about Britishness may illustrate this. He said:

> *"They, (the British) hate me, and I hate 'em back".*

If not careful, the mutual exclusion and the exclusion of the person itself, could add to the context of recent human tragedies and would surely keep deepening differences among groups. This could maintain the perception in both groups (immigrants and nationals) as "unfamiliar" to each other, and fatally separating them form each other.

Another assertion supporting the similar effects of the high committed members of a group is the one mentioned by Olivier Roy (2004), who studied Muslim radicals seeking to explain how categorization processes related to religion, may fuel intentions of radical people to identify with categories defined by agents external to western society. A categorization that is easily used to manipulate the identity of Islamic by fanatics is the way they perceive their "membership to the Umma" [or Muslim brotherhood]. This is a worldwide supra-identity, that by occupying an important place in an individual's identity, can easily displace the "Common Dutchness" which is proposed here. Reactions originated from fear to threat of "others" to this "Muslim Supra Identity" could give way to the sense of being different from the rest of Dutch people. As consequence, retribution or revenge may become the evident consequence of this type of supra identities and the way they relate to out-group members .

As the theories in this work suggest as a way for avoiding groups conflicts, it could happen that - like it has happened before in the Netherlands - the differences between groups would diminish, and immigrants could be eventually accepted as nationals. However, the opposite may be possible when threatening situations endure and differences between people are made salient every time.

The Netherlands has been called an "immigration country", but it is necessary to say that the arrival of new immigrant groups will keep causing new conflicts. The newest immigrant groups may then become "black sheep", causing the feelings of threat between an "older immigrant group" and the Dutch to diminish. The new groups of immigrants could become "the new common out-group", externally targeted by the groups which were earlier in conflict. The rearrangement and re-categorization of groups may be causes for the feelings of threat to diminish, being redirected or even disappearing. They could disappear in the way zuilings did (*Kağıdışi* 1994), followed by accentuation of the "otherness" and the difference of these minorities from the majority population. Roccas et al. (2002) have affirmed this, when they observed that tolerance to other groups is related to the "buffering effect" of the complexity of identity. Instead of pointing at the different verzuilingen, Roccas et al. (2002) have proposed the creation of the awareness of the (Dutch) "in-group diversity", which can be translated into the inclusion of "all zuilingen (or pillars)" as the way to ease tensions. This re-defining of a more complex definition of the Dutch identity needs to include the question of what is the in-group?, as well as requiring the definition of what the group is not. This awakes a real need to do this constantly, re-defining in a new inclusive way what it means to have a "Dutch Identity". Adding characteristics of new groups to the national identity will help the inhabitant of the Netherlands feel that they can contribute to the formation of a richer identity and can incorporate them into this "supra self-concept" of being Dutch.

Hundred of thousands of immigrants who now reside in the Netherlands have undergone a process of reconstruction of their self-identity during the last decades. Because of the openness that they show to change their identity, it may be less difficult to incorporate their identity with the proposed new category of "Dutchness". It may be just necessary to offer this to them, not only through conferring them legal documents, but with the invitation to "redefine the Dutch identity." This may require a national agreement, which involves incorporating the new elements of culture to what it mean to be a "Hollander" in these times. Doing this may help attach positive affects and emotions–or at least lower the levels of anxiety- to the diverse members of their in-group. Conflict will then be seen as an in-group situation, and may be reduced using strategies such as decategorization, recategorization and subcategorization. The process should be presented as subordinated to the super-ordinated idea of becoming Dutch. It will require willingness and consent from the Dutch Nationals, as well as cooperative efforts, promotion of cooperation between groups and compensation of the groups' statuses. Doing this will lead to unity and the overcoming of inter-group conflicts, which will defeat the feelings of threat to identity.

The promoting of a "common Dutchness" could make this identity more prominent to minorities groups, strengthening the notion of citizenship. The promotion of integration of group elements of identity into the greater picture of society is different than requiring the individual to choose for just one identity. As indicated by the Social Identity Theory, it is possible for human beings to adopt more than one identity, without necessarily having to see them as contradictory or causing conflict. The opening of alternative frameworks (or identities) in which people and their groups could feel more at home contribute to the ongoing homogenization of society, therefore helping in the forming of harmonious group relations. This is not an 'instant solution' to group tensions, but a gradual process to improve inter-group relations.

A new attachment of emotional significance given by all groups in the constitution of the whole could open doors for a better understanding of the immigrant groups in Dutch society, and their participation in it. This promotion of a sense of inclusion could make the new groups feel that they can be categorized as part of the national "meta-identity". As a consequence of feeling Dutch, any threat to this "common Dutch identity" will be felt by the new immigrant groups as well.

For what it has been described in this work, having low commitment members of out-groups coming to the nation will be – at least- apparently – a good way to produce successful orientation towards other groups in the country. But this may result also in a counterproductive situation for the particular subjects, since they will show preference to out-groups rather than towards their own group. This approach will not prevent intergroup conflicts. The disposition of immigrant groups for not to wanting to maintain their cultural identity in order to assimilate into the "majority's culture could lead towards negative results in the acculturation strategy adopted by individuals. This way of trying to hold on to new intergroup contacts could cause feelings of betrayal to the roots of the identities in the members of immigrants groups. The result of such approach will be a kind of "marginalization of individuals" from both, their in-group and others' groups. Meanwhile, the opposite situation would be more desirable, keeping individuals in contact with their own group's identity as well as a daily interaction with other groups belonging to the Dutch social net of relations. It appears relevant to mention here that the increment of social interaction also helps increasing pro-social behavior among individuals. The social interaction should be intentional, but not intensive, because as Insko, Kirtchner, Pinter, Efaw and Wildschut (2004, in Penner, Dovidio, Pilavin and Schroeder, 2004) have warned, pro-social behavior generates increasing levels on competition among the groups when emphasizing a general common identity of the groups.

With all what it has been written in this work, it is necessary to admit that the subject of inter-group relations in the Netherlands is extensive. This allows for the rise of new theories and proposals to answer questions such as: How could the manipulation of the commitment to a group affect the intergroup dynamics of its members?; In which ways important identity elements of immigrants (such as language, customs, etc.) could be transformed or replaced by elements that are relevant to the Dutch culture? In which ways important identity elements of immigrants could be made relevant to the Dutch culture. Further research is necessary to answer this questions. It would also be interesting to do research about the effects of the current technologic environment (such as internet, virtual locations, satellite) and globalization on the different human identities as well as how it affects intergroup relations.

Finally; individuals and groups will always find differences that can cause feelings of threat towards each other, but the amazing flexibility of the human race, demonstrated in how an individual can negotiate different identities in different situations, remains a valuable gift and ability that can ease difficult circumstances. This gift, if used wisely, could prevent national conflicts and escalations.

The Netherlands has an extensive history of positive contact with different groups through the ages. Taking advantage of its history, added to the richness of the cultural diversity in this nation, are sufficiently strong reasons to offer an optimistic view of its social relations, while trying to make groups in the country realize that *"We" versus "Them" equals "Us"*.

BIBLIOGRAPHY

Abrams, D., & Hutchison, D. (2002). *From paragon to pariah: How groups react to deviance and extremity among their members.* Paper presented at the British Psychological Society's Annual Conference, Blackpool, 13 – 15 March, in Demoulin, S.; Rodriguez Torres, R.; Rodriguez Perez; A.; Vaez, J, Paladino , M. P., Gaunt, R., Cortes Pozo, B & Leyens, J.P. (2004) Emotional prejudice can lead to infra-humanisation. *European Review of Social Psychology.* **15**, 259–296.

Berry, J.W., Poortinga, Y.H., Segall, M.H., & Dasen, P.R. (2002). *Cross-cultural psychology: Research and applications.* (2nd Ed.). Cambridge, UK: Cambridge University Press.

Branscombe, N.R., & Spears, R. (2001). Social psychology: Past, present, and some predictions for the future. In J.S. Halonen & S.F. Davis (Eds.), *The many faces of psychological research in the 21st century.* Syracuse, NY: Society for the Teaching of Psychology. (on internet at: http://teachpsych.lemoyne.edu/teachpsych/faces/script/Ch07.htm)

Brendsen M., Van der Pligt, J. Doosje, B., & Manstead A. (2004) Guilt and regreet: The determining role of interpersonal and intrapresonal harm. *Cognition and Emotion,* **18** (1), 55-70.

Brown, R. (2000) Social Identity Theory: Past achievements, current problems and future challenges. *European Jourmnal of Social Psychology.* **30**, 745-778.

Castano, E., Yzerbyt, V., Bourguignon, D., & Serón, E. (2002). Who may enter? The impact of in-group Identification on in-group/out-group categorization. *Journal of Experimental Social Psychology* , **38**, 315-322.

Castles, S. *Ethnicity and Globalization,* London, Sage, 2000.

Celious A. and Oyserman Daphna (2001). Race From Inside: An Emerging Heterogeneous Race Model. *Journal of Social Issues*, **57**(1): pp149-165.

Cialdini, R.B. , & Kendrik, D.T. (1976) Altruism as hedonism: A social development perspective on the relationship of negative mood state and helping. *Journal of Personality and social Psychology*, **34**. 907-914.

Doosje, B., & Kateman, S. (2004). Ethnic Attitudes after september 11th: The Role of personal group threat and fear., The Netherlands. *Department of Social Psychology, University of Amsterdam.*

Doosje, B. Branscombe, N.R., & Manstead, A.S. R. (1998). Guilt by association: When one's group has a negative history. *Journal of Personality and Social Psychology*, **75**: 872-886.

Dovidio, J.F., Gaertner, S.L., & Kawakami, K. (2003) Intergroup contact: past, present and future. *Group Processes and intergroup Relations.* **6** (1): 5-21.

Ellemers, N, Spears, R., & Doosje, B. (2002). Self and social identity. *Annual Review of Psychology,* **53**: 161-186.

Ellemers N., Kortekaas, P., & Ouwerkerk J.W.(1999) Self categorisation, commitment to the group and group self-esteem as related but distinct aspects of social identity. *European Journal of Social Psychology,* **29,** 371-389.

Deaux; Kay (2000) Surveying the Landscape of immigration: Social Psychological Perspectives. *Journal of Community and Applied Social Psychology,* **10**:421-431.

Dumont, M., Yzerbyt, V., Wigboldus, D., & Gordijn, E.H.(2003) Social categorization and fear reactions to the september 11th Terrorist Attacks. *Personality and Social Psychology bulletin.* **9** (12): 1509-20

Entzinger, H.B. & Stijnen, P.J.J. (Eds.), Etnische minderheden in Nederland. Meppel - Heerlen: Boom. Open Universiteit - Nederland.

Farham, S.D., Greeenwald, A.G. , & Banaji, M.R. (1999) In D.Abrams & M. Hogg (Eds.) *Social identity and social cognition* (pp230-248). Oxford, UK: Blackwell.

Gaertner, S., Dovidio, J., Anastasio, P., Bachman, B., & Rust, M. (1993). The Common Ingroup Identity Model:

Recategorization and the reduction of intergroup bias. In W. Stroebe and M. Hewstone (Eds.), *European Review of Social Psychology*, (pp.1-26). New York, NY: Wiley & Sons.

Green, D.P., Glaser, J., & Rich, A. (1998). From lynching to gay-bashing: The elusive connection between economic conditions and hate crime. *Journal of Personality and Social Psychology*. **75**: 82-92.

Gijsberts, M., & Dagevos, J. (2005). Uit elkaars buurt: De invloed van etnische concentratie op integratie en beeldvorming. *Sociaal en Cultureel Planbureau*, Den Haag. The Netherlands.

Haslam S. A., Powell, C. & Turner, J. (2000). Social identity, self-categorization, and work motivation: Rethinking the contribution of the group to positive and sustainable organizational outcomes. *Applied Psychology An International Review*, 49, (3), pp. 319-339(21).

Haslam, S. Alexander, Penelope J. Oakes, Katherine J. Reynolds and John C. Turner (1999). "Social Identity Salience and the Emergence of Stereotype Consensus." *Personality and Social Psychology Bulletin*. **25** (7): 809-818.

Hewstone, M., Rubin, M., & Willis, H. (2002). Intergroup bias. *Annual Review of Psychology*. **53**:575-604

Hogg, M.A., Abrams, D., Otten, S., & Hinkle, S. (2004) The Social Identity Perspective: intergroup relations-

conception, and small groups. *Small Group Research.* **35** (3): 246–76.

Hogg, M. A., & Abrams, D. (1988). *Social identifications: A social psychology of intergroup relations and group processes.* London: Routledge.

Hopkins, N. and Murdock, N. (1999) The Role of the 'Other' in National Identity: Exploring the Context-dependence of the National Ingroup Stereotype. *Journal of Community and Applied Social Psychology;* **9**:321-338.

Jacobson, J. Perception of Britishness (1997). *Nations and nationalism.* **3** (2), 181-199

Jetten, J., Spears, R.,& Manstead, A. S. R. (1999). Group distinctiveness and intergroup discrimination. In N. Ellemers, R. Spears,& B. Doosje (Eds.), *Social identity: Context, commitment, content* (pp. 107–126). Oxford, England: Blackwell.

Jetten J., & Spears R. (1997). Distinctiveness threat and prototypically: combined effects on intergroup discrimination and collective self-esteem. *European Journal of Social Psychology;* **27**: 635-657 .

Jetten J., Postmes, T., & Mcaulife, B.J. (2002). We are all individuals: Group norms of individualism and collectivism, levels of identification and identity threat. *European Journal of Social Psychology.* **32**, 189-207.

Kağiçişi (1994) Paper presented at a symposium on "Nationalism and Ethnocentrism: A Priority Puzzle for Psychology" (organized by M.B. Smith) at the *23rd International Congress of Applied Psychology*, Madrid, July 17–22, 1994.

Karasawa M., Karasawa, K., & Hirose , Y. (2004) Homogeneity perception as a reaction to identity threat: Effects of status difference in a simulated society game. *European Journal of Social Psychology.* **34**, 613-625.

Leach , C.W., & Williams, W. R.. (1999) Group Identity and Conflict Expectations of the future in Northern Ireland, 1999. *International Society of Political Psychology.* **20**, 4, 1999.

Licata L., & Klein O. (2002) Does European citizenship breed Xenophobia? European Identification as predictor of intolerance towards immigrants. *Community and Applied Social Psychology* **12**:323-337 .

Lindeman Marjaana (1997) Ingroup bias, self – enhancement and group identification. *European Journal of Social Psychology.* **27**: 337-355.

Meertens, R.W., & Pettigrew, T. (1997) Is subtle prejudice really prejudice?. *Public Opinion Quarterly.* **61**, 54-71.

Muslims in the EU: Cities Report, The Netherlands. Preliminary research report and literature survey. pp. 22-23. *Open Society Institute - EU Monitoring and Advocacy Program (EUMAP) (2007).*

Oliver Roy, Globalized Islam . Columbia Univ. Press, New York, 2004.

Onishi, A. and Murphy-Shigematsu, S. (2003). Identity Narratives of Muslim Foreign Workers in Japan. *Journal of Community and Applied Social Psychology*, **13**.224-239.

Ottaway, S. A., Hayden, D. C. & Oakes, M. A. (2001). Implicit attitudes and racism: Effect of word familiarity and frequency on the Implicit Association Test. *Social Cognition*. **19**, 97– 144.

Pettigrew, T.F. (1998). Reactions toward the new minorities in Europe. *Annual Review of Sociology*. **24**, 77-103.

Pettigrew, T., & Meertens, R.W. (1996). The verzuiling puzzle: understanding Dutch intergroup relations. *Current Psychology*, **15** (1) 0737-8262. (on internet: Bussiness Sourcec Premier)

Penner, L.A., Dovidio, J.F., Pilavin, J.A., and Schroeder, D.A. (2004). Prosocial Behavior: Multilevel Perspectives. AR Reviews in Advance. *Annual Review of Psychology*. **56** , 14.1-14-28.

Roccas, S. & Brewer M.(2002). Social identity complexity. *Personality and Social Psychology Review*. **6** (2): 88-106.

Schachter, S. (1959). *The psychology of affiliation*. Stanford, CA: Stanford University Press.

Scheepers D., Spears, R., Doosje, B., & Manstead, A. S. R. (2003). Two functions of verbal intergroup discrimination: Identity and instrumental motives as a result of group identification and threat. *Personality and Social Psychology Bulletin.* **29** (5): 568-577.

Schmitt M.T.; & Branscombe N. R. (2001). The Good, the bad, and the manly: Threats to one's prototypicality and evaluations of fellow in group members. *Experimental Social Psychology.* **37**, 510-517).

Smith , H.J., & Leach. C. W. (2004). Group Membership and everyday social comparison experiences. *European Journal of Social Psychology.* **34**: 297-308.

Spiecker, B. , & Steutel Jan (2001) Multiculturalism, pillarization and liberal civic education in the Netherlands. *International Journal of Educational Research.* **35**: 293-304.

Stephan, W. G., Stephan, C. W. & Gudykunst, W. (1999). Anxiety in intergroup relations: A
comparison of anxiety/uncertainty management theory and integrated threat theory. *International Journal of Intercultural Relations.* **23**: 4, 613-628.

Tajfel, H. and Turner, J. C. (1986). The social identity theory of inter-group behavior. In S. Worchel and L. W. Austin (eds.), *Psychology of Intergroup Relations.* Chigago: Nelson-Hall.

Timotijevic, L., & Breakwell, G.M. (2000) Migration threat to identity. *Journal of Community & Applied Social Psychology*. **10**: 335-372.

Turner, J. C. (1982). Towards a cognitive redefinition of the social group. In H. Tajfel (ed.), *Social Identity and Intergroup Relations*. Cambridge: Cambridge University Press.

Turner, R.G. (1978a). Consistency, self-consciousness, and the predictive validity of typical and maximal personality measures. *Journal of Research in Personality* . **12**: 117-132.

Turner, R.G. (1978b). Self-consciousness and speed of processing self-relevant information. *Journal of Research in Personality*. **12**: 431-438

Verkuyten, M. (2004) Everyday ways of thinking about multiculturalism. *Ethnicities*. 1468-7968, **4** (1): 53-74.

Verkuyten, M. (2001). ' Abnormalization' of ethnic minorities in conversation. *British Journal of Social Psychology*. **40**: 257-2783.

Vignoles, V.L., Chyssochoou, X., & Breakwell, G. (2000). The distinctiveness principle: Identity meaning, and the bounds of cultural relativeness. *Personality and Social Psychology Review*. **4**: 337-354.